United States Government Accountability Office

Report to the Ranking Member,
Committee on the Budget, U.S. Senate

I0455235

September 2013

BIOMEDICAL RESEARCH

NIH Should Assess the Impact of Growth in Indirect Costs on Its Mission

BIOMEDICAL RESEARCH

NIH Should Assess the Impact of Growth in Indirect Costs on Its Mission

GAO Highlights

Highlights of GAO-13-760, a report to the Ranking Member, Committee on the Budget, U.S. Senate

Why GAO Did This Study

NIH reimburses universities for both the direct and indirect costs of conducting research. Indirect costs cover general facility and administrative expenses, and are paid as a percentage, or rate, of certain direct costs of awarded grants. GAO was asked to look at the indirect costs of NIH-funded research. This report (1) identifies changes in reimbursements by NIH to universities for indirect costs of NIH-funded research; and (2) examines key factors affecting NIH reimbursement to universities for indirect costs and what assessment NIH has done to address any impact of these costs on NIH's research mission. GAO analyzed NIH data and interviewed officials at NIH, six universities, and other stakeholders. Universities were selected based on the number of grants and amount of funding received from NIH and their negotiated indirect cost rates.

What GAO Recommends

GAO recommends that NIH assess the impact of growth in indirect costs on its mission, including, as necessary, planning for how to deal with potential future increases in indirect costs that could limit the amount of funding available for total research. HHS agreed with GAO's recommendation but disagreed with a number of GAO's conclusions, stating that risk to NIH's mission is low because indirect costs remain a stable percentage of NIH's budget. Due to indications that indirect costs for universities may increase in the future, GAO believes that continually assessing and planning for the impact of growth over the long term is important.

View GAO-13-760. For more information, contact Linda T. Kohn at (202) 512-7114 or kohnl@gao.gov.

What GAO Found

From fiscal year 2002 to fiscal year 2012, indirect cost reimbursements from the National Institutes of Health (NIH) to universities increased slightly faster than those for direct costs, but increased notably faster during some periods. Specifically, from fiscal years 2002 to 2012, indirect costs increased 28.1 percent while direct costs increased 27.0 percent. However, for the fiscal years 2003 to 2012, indirect costs increased notably faster than direct costs, at 16.9 percent and 11.7 percent, respectively. In more recent years, annual changes were generally small but consistent. This increase occurred during a time when growth in NIH's budget for extramural research slowed to 5 percent from fiscal years 2008 to 2012, compared to about 21 percent from fiscal years 2002 to 2007. In fiscal year 2012, about 10 percent of the universities (50 out of about 500) receiving NIH extramural research funding received almost 70 percent of all indirect cost reimbursement provided to universities. Higher indirect cost rates tended to be associated with universities located in high-cost-of-living areas and privately owned universities.

Stakeholders—university officials, Department of Health and Human Services (HHS) officials, and others—whom GAO interviewed identified several key factors that may lead to increases in reimbursements for indirect costs provided to universities. Some stakeholders reported that reimbursements for one part of indirect costs—the facilities component—help to support research innovation by providing funding for the development and maintenance of state-of-the-art research facilities. However, officials in HHS's Division of Cost Allocation, which is responsible for determining indirect cost rates, stated that the uncapped facilities component of the indirect cost rate provides universities with few, if any, incentives for controlling these costs. For example, these officials noted that there is no limit on reimbursement for interest costs under the facilities component. This may encourage universities to borrow money to build new facilities, which could lead to building more new space than is necessary for research. Some stakeholders also noted that a 26 percent cap on the reimbursement rate for administrative costs—a second component of indirect costs—helps to control reimbursements for those costs; however, they reported it does not account for the recent increases in costs, such as those for regulatory reporting requirements and changing research needs that require advanced medical and information technologies that are considered administrative.

The combination of these trends and factors results in indirect costs growing at a faster rate than direct costs. Indirect costs are one-fifth of NIH's total budget—or $6.2 billion in fiscal year 2012—but NIH officials reported that they have not taken steps to assess the significance of future indirect cost growth for universities, or planned for options that might address these trends or factors—in part because they view increases in indirect costs as having been modest. However, factors suggest that indirect costs could increase more quickly in the future. Over the long term, they could lead to a reduction in the number of research grants that could be funded, thus potentially affecting scientific discoveries and knowledge.

Contents

Letter		1
	Background	5
	From 2002 to 2012, NIH Indirect Cost Reimbursements to Universities Increased Faster than for Direct Costs, with Most Going to a Small Number of Universities	11
	Stakeholders Identified Factors Related to Facilities and Administrative Costs That May Increase Reimbursements for Indirect Costs, but NIH Has Not Assessed Their Potential Impact	16
	Conclusions	19
	Recommendation	20
	Agency Comments and Our Evaluation	20

Appendix I	Indirect Costs and Rates for the Top 50 National Institutes of Health—Funded Universities, Fiscal Year 2012	23

Appendix II	Comments from the Department of Health and Human Services	25

Appendix III	GAO Contact and Staff Acknowledgments	31

Table		
	Table 1: Characteristics of the 10 Universities with the Highest Indirect Cost Rates among the 50 Universities Receiving the Highest Amounts of Indirect Cost Reimbursement, Fiscal Year 2012	15

Figures		
	Figure 1: Total Direct Costs and Modified Total Direct Costs	9
	Figure 2: Percent Change from the Prior Year in Reimbursement for Direct and Indirect Costs, Fiscal Year 2003 to Fiscal Year 2012	12

Abbreviations

DCA	Division of Cost Allocation
DOD	Department of Defense
HHS	Department of Health and Human Services
IC	institutes and centers
IT	information technology
MTDC	modified total direct costs
NIH	National Institutes of Health
OMB	Office of Management and Budget
ONR	Office of Naval Research

This is a work of the U.S. government and is not subject to copyright protection in the United States. The published product may be reproduced and distributed in its entirety without further permission from GAO. However, because this work may contain copyrighted images or other material, permission from the copyright holder may be necessary if you wish to reproduce this material separately.

September 24, 2013

The Honorable Jeff Sessions
Ranking Member
Committee on the Budget
United States Senate

Dear Senator Sessions:

The federal government has recognized that research conducted at universities contributes to American competitiveness and leadership in science and has committed to sponsoring a share of the research costs.[1] The Department of Health and Human Services' (HHS) National Institutes of Health (NIH) is the nation's leader in conducting and sponsoring biomedical research. A large portion of this research is extramural research conducted at universities nationwide, which is an essential part of how NIH fulfills its mission—to understand the nature and behavior of living systems and to improve health. In fiscal year 2012, $25.2 billion—or over 80 percent of NIH's budget of $30.8 billion—was used to support extramural research. NIH reimburses universities for both the direct and the indirect costs of conducting biomedical research. Direct costs can be specifically attributed to research projects sponsored by NIH grants, including costs for labor and materials used solely to carry out sponsored research. Indirect costs are not directly attributable to a specific project and include various facility and administrative expenses incurred by the universities for the shared support of such research. Indirect costs represented approximately $6.2 billion in fiscal year 2012, or 20 percent of NIH's budget.

To be reimbursed for direct and indirect costs, universities must properly identify and claim reimbursement for these costs in accordance with applicable federal guidance. Office of Management and Budget (OMB) Circular No. A-21 establishes the principles for determining the types of direct and indirect costs that are allowed to be claimed and the methods for allocating such costs to federally funded research at educational

---

[1]For the purposes of this report, the term "universities" refers to domestic higher education institutions.

institutions.[2] Because indirect costs cannot be specifically attributed to a particular research grant, they are charged via an indirect cost rate that is applied to certain direct costs for each awarded grant.[3] Each university negotiates an indirect cost rate, based on information such as the amount of physical space used for conducting research. Most universities negotiate their indirect cost rate with HHS's Division of Cost Allocation (DCA).[4] Generally, the rate stays in effect for 2 to 4 years, at which time a new proposal is developed and the rate is renegotiated. Once a university's indirect cost rate has been established, a federal agency will generally apply that rate to all grants issued to that university.[5]

All federal agencies, including NIH, are responsible for implementing internal controls to, among other things, provide reasonable assurance that the agency is achieving its goals by operating in an effective and efficient manner.[6] A key element of internal control is risk assessment, which is the identification and analysis of relevant risks associated with achieving the agency's objectives. As we previously reported, NIH has a program to periodically identify, analyze, and manage significant risks to its objectives, strategy and mission.[7] Since NIH achieves its mission largely through extramural research, the indirect and the direct costs of

---

[2]Office of Management and Budget, *Cost Principles for Educational Institutions*, OMB Circular No. A-21 ((incorporated in 2 C.F.R. 220) (2012)).

[3]The indirect cost rate is applied to certain direct costs—referred to as "modified total direct costs" (MTDC). For MTDC, certain direct costs or portions of direct costs are excluded from total direct costs, such as equipment costs. For example, for a grant award with total direct costs of $110,000, a MTDC of $100,000, and an indirect cost rate of 50 percent, NIH would reimburse the university $50,000 for the indirect costs of research for a total grant award of $160,000.

[4]OMB Circular No. A-21 assigns responsibility to negotiate rates to either HHS or the Department of Defense (DOD). (OMB Circular A-21, G, 11, a, (1).) DCA handles this responsbility within HHS, and the Office of Naval Research (ONR) does so for DOD. As of 2010, DCA is responsible for negotiating rates with more than 1,000 universities, while ONR is responsible for 44 universities.

[5]While OMB Circular No. A-21 requires agencies to adhere to the negotiated rate while it is in effect, an agency may apply a different rate when required by law or regulation. (OMB Circular A-21, G,11, b.)

[6]See GAO, *Standards for Internal Control in the Federal Government*, GAO/AIMD-00-21.3.1 (Washington, D.C.: Nov. 1, 1999).

[7]See GAO, *National Institutes of Health: Completion of Comprehensive Risk Management Program Essential to Effective Oversight*, GAO-09-687 (Washington, D.C.: Sept. 11, 2009).

extramural research have the potential to affect NIH's ability to achieve its objectives and mission.

We have previously reported that indirect costs can change over time and that indirect cost rates at universities varied widely.[8] Furthermore, we have noted that there has been debate over what portion of indirect costs is the responsibility of the government and what portion is the responsibility of the university.[9] Given our past work, you requested that we provide information on the indirect costs for NIH-funded extramural research. In this report, we

1. identify changes in the reimbursements paid by NIH to universities to support indirect costs of NIH-funded research and examine the characteristics of the top recipients of this funding, such as the type of institution and the geographic location; and

2. examine the key factors affecting reimbursement to universities for the indirect costs of NIH-funded research and what assessment NIH has done to address any impact of these costs on NIH's research mission.

To identify changes in the reimbursements paid by NIH to universities to support the indirect costs of NIH-funded research and examine the characteristics of the top recipients of this funding, we obtained information from NIH on the total amounts of direct and indirect costs paid to universities for NIH research grants over the past decade (from fiscal year 2002 through fiscal year 2012).[10] We analyzed the data provided by NIH and identified the top universities—those receiving the most NIH indirect cost funding—as well as the various characteristics associated with these universities. We also obtained and reviewed data from HHS's DCA on the indirect cost rates for almost 300 universities that received NIH research grant funding from fiscal year 2002 through fiscal year

---

[8]See GAO, *National Institutes of Health Extramural Research Grants: Oversight of Cost Reimbursements to Universities,* GAO-07-294R (Washington, D.C.: January 31, 2007); and *University Research: Policies for the Reimbursement of Indirect Costs Need to Be Updated,* GAO-10-937 (Washington, D.C.: Sept. 8, 2010).

[9]See GAO-10-937.

[10]Our analysis focused on the relative differences between changes for indirect cost reimbursements and direct cost reimbursements. Therefore, we do not adjust the changes in reimbursements for inflation.

2012.[11] We reviewed the indirect cost rates among the top universities and identified various characteristics—such as the local cost of living index, the type of institution, and the geographic location—associated with those universities.

To assess the reliability of NIH's grant funding data (including the data on direct and indirect cost funding), we reviewed our prior work using these data and obtained information from agency officials knowledgeable about the reliability of the data. We performed data quality checks to assess the reliability of the data received from both NIH and DCA. These data quality checks involved an assessment to identify missing or incorrect entries or outliers. Based on the information we obtained and analyses we conducted, we determined that the data we used were sufficiently reliable for the purposes of this report.

In addition, we interviewed stakeholders—including officials with (1) NIH, (2) DCA, (3) the Council on Governmental Relations, an association of academic research institutions, (4) the Association of American Universities, and (5) 6 selected universities—about the amount of funding and key characteristics of the 50 universities receiving the highest reimbursements for indirect costs. We selected the 6 universities from among the top 50 recipients of NIH indirect cost funding to include universities that varied in terms of their (1) amount of indirect cost funding received; (2) current negotiated indirect cost rate; (3) number of grants received; (4) local cost of living; and (5) type of university (public versus privately funded).[12] We focused on the top 50 universities because they are responsible for about two thirds of NIH research conducted at universities.[13]

---

[11]We obtained and reviewed data for approximately 300 "long-form universities," which are those universities that use a "long form" during negotiations with DCA because their total federal funding is greater than $10 million per year.

[12]For indirect cost funding amount, indirect cost rate, and the number of grants, we used fiscal year 2012 data. For cost of living, we used the U.S. Census Bureau's "cost of living index" for 2010.

[13]Our review does not include nonuniversity grantees (such as nonacademic research institutions) that received NIH grant funding.

To examine the key factors affecting reimbursement to universities for the indirect costs of NIH-funded research and what assessment NIH has done to address any impact of these costs on NIH's research mission, we reviewed relevant laws, policies, and guidance, and interviewed relevant officials. Documents we reviewed included OMB Circular No. A-21—which establishes principles on how the federal government reimburses universities for the costs of federally funded research—and HHS and NIH guidance related to the process for reviewing and negotiating indirect cost rate and providing reimbursement of direct and indirect costs. We also reviewed proposed revisions to current policies for reimbursement of indirect costs issued by OMB and literature from stakeholders that include potential changes to address reported disadvantages of current policies, and alternative approaches to current policies for providing reimbursement for indirect costs. In addition, we interviewed officials from HHS's DCA and NIH about how they implement policies on indirect costs, how reported key factors could affect NIH's funding of future research, and what assessment NIH has done to address trends in indirect costs. We also conducted interviews with private grant-making foundations that support biomedical research to determine their policies on reimbursement of indirect costs.

We conducted this performance audit from February 2013 to September 2013, in accordance with generally accepted government auditing standards. Those standards require that we plan and perform the audit to obtain sufficient, appropriate evidence to provide a reasonable basis for our findings and conclusions based on our audit objectives. We believe that the evidence obtained provides a reasonable basis for our findings and conclusions based on our audit objectives.

Background

NIH conducts and sponsors biomedical research through its institutes and centers (IC), each of which is charged with a specific mission. ICs' missions generally focus on a given disease; a particular organ; or a stage in development, such as childhood or old age. ICs accomplish their missions chiefly through intramural and extramural research. Intramural research entails government scientists working in the ICs' own laboratories and clinics, whereas extramural research is conducted at outside research institutions, primarily universities, by scientists who have been awarded extramural research grants from an IC through NIH's competitive process.[14] More than 80 percent of NIH's total budget of over $30 billion in fiscal year 2012 was used to support extramural research. Of this $25.2 billion in extramural research grant funding, NIH provided about $16.1 billion to universities.

Components of Direct and Indirect Costs

Extramural research grants reimburse universities for the direct costs of each research project covered by the grants and a portion of the indirect costs of maintaining their facilities for research use and covering the administrative expenses of the university. Direct costs can be specifically identified with or directly assigned to individual research projects and are relatively easy to define and measure.[15] They include, for example, the researcher's salary, subawards,[16] equipment, and travel.[17] Indirect costs represent a university's general support expenses and cannot be specifically identified with individual research projects or institutional activities. They include, for example, building utilities, administrative staff salaries, and library operations. OMB Circular No. A-21 establishes the principles for determining the types of direct and indirect costs that are allowed to be claimed and the methods for allocating such costs to federally funded research at educational institutions, including the establishment and use of indirect cost rates.[18]

---

[14]For more information on NIH funding provided to universities, see GAO-07-249R.

[15]*See* OMB Circular No. A-21, D,1.

[16]A subaward is an award provided by a recipient of a federal award to another researcher, for the performance of substantive work under the federal award.

[17]Certain direct costs or portions of direct costs are excluded when estimating indirect cost rates. Examples of these exclusions are equipment and portions of subawards in excess of $25,000.

[18]OMB Circular No. A-21 requires all costs for reimbursement to be allowable, allocable, and reasonable, and provides that the federal government bear its fair share of total costs, determined in accordance with generally accepted accounting principles, except where restricted or prohibited by law. A cost is allowable if it is reasonable, is allocable to the agreement, is treated consistently with generally accepted accounting principles appropriate to the circumstances, and conforms to principles in OMB Circular No. A-21 and the sponsoring agreement. A cost may be considered reasonable if the nature of the goods or services acquired or applied, and the amount involved, reflect the action that a prudent person would have taken under the circumstances prevailing at the time the decision to incur the cost was made. A cost is allocable to a particular cost objective (i.e., a specific function, project, sponsored agreement, department, or the like) if the goods or services involved are chargeable or assignable to such cost objective in accordance with relative benefits received or other equitable relationship. (OMB Circular No. A-21, C.)

Indirect costs are divided into two main components, facilities costs and administrative costs. Facilities costs include

- operations and maintenance expenses, such as for utilities;[19]

- allowances for depreciation and use of buildings and equipment;

- interest on debt associated with building and equipment; and

- library expenses, such as for the use of the library and library materials purchased for research use.

Administrative costs include

- general administration expenses, such as the costs associated with executive functions like financial management;

- departmental administration expenses, including clerical staff and supplies for academic departments;

- sponsored projects' administration expenses, which are the costs associated with the office responsible for administering projects and awards funded by external sources; and

- student administration and services expenses, such as the administration of the student health clinic.

Calculation of the Indirect Cost Rate

Because indirect costs cannot be specifically attributed to a particular research grant, they are charged via an indirect cost rate that serves as the mechanism for determining the proportion of indirect costs that may be charged to federally funded research awards. OMB Circular No. A-21 outlines the process for establishing an indirect cost rate for universities performing federally funded research. Each university develops a proposed indirect cost rate that is based on university cost data from prior years, which is subsequently negotiated with the federal government to

---

[19]Certain universities are eligible for a rate increase of 1.3 percent to account for the cost of utilities—known as the utility cost adjustment.

arrive at a final indirect cost rate, in compliance with the principles of OMB Circular A-21.[20]

To calculate a university's indirect cost rate, a percentage of each indirect cost component is allocated to the university's research function on the basis of benefits received from that component by the research function. For example, a university can measure the square footage of floor space used for research and use this measure to allocate the amount of costs it claims for operating and using the space as a component in its indirect cost rate proposal. Each indirect cost component allocated to research is applied to a modified set of direct costs referred to as "modified total direct costs" (MTDC) to obtain an individual rate for each component.[21] MTDC includes the salaries and wages of those conducting the research, fringe benefits (e.g., pensions), materials and supplies, travel, and the first $25,000 of each subaward. MTDC excludes costs such as equipment costs, capital expenditures, tuition remission,[22] equipment or space rental costs, and the portion of each subaward in excess of $25,000.[23] (See fig. 1.)

---

[20]While OMB Circular No. A-21 requires agencies to adhere to the negotiated rate while it is in effect, an agency may apply a different rate when required by law or regulation. (OMB Circular A-21, G,11, b.)

[21]Universities use a standard format, also known as the long form, for submitting their indirect cost rate proposals to their cognizant rate-setting agency. However, universities whose total direct costs on federal awards do not exceed $10 million in a fiscal year may use a simplified method for determining the indirect cost rate applicable to all federal awards. Whereas universities above the $10 million threshold must use an MTDC base, universities using the simplified method may use either salaries and wages as their base, or MTDC. As already noted, this report focuses on those universities that used the standard format for proposal submission.

[22]Tuition remission is compensation provided to graduate research assistants in lieu of salary.

[23]Costs for subawards over $25,000 and equipment are excluded because they can involve very large expenditures but usually do not require the university's facilities and administrative support.

Figure 1: Total Direct Costs and Modified Total Direct Costs

Total direct costs (TDC) =
Sum of direct costs specifically
identified with particular
projects or activities

- Subawards
- Equipment
- Researcher salary

For MTDC, certain direct costs or
portions of direct costs are excluded
from TDC

Examples of exclusions:
- Equipment
- Portion of subawards in excess of
  $25,000

Modified total direct costs
(MTDC)

Exclusions

TDC

MTDC = TDC - Exclusions

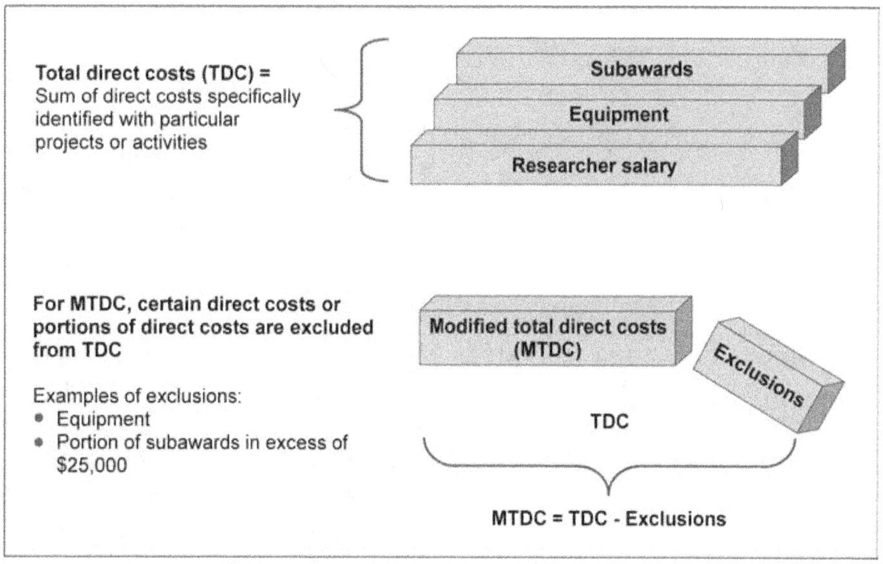

Source: GAO analysis of OMB Circular A-21.

The indirect cost rate is developed as follows:

- Each portion of the facilities costs (i.e., building use, depreciation, operations and maintenance) is divided by MTDC and then added together to derive the facilities component of the rate.

- Similarly, each portion of the administrative costs (i.e., general administration, sponsored administration) is divided by MTDC and then added together to derive the administrative component of the rate—which is capped at 26 percent.

- These individual rates—the facilities and administrative—are then summed to obtain the university's indirect cost rate for research.

In 1991, OMB revised Circular No. A-21 to impose a cap of 26 percent on the administrative component of the indirect cost rate. This cap was established to curb growth in the amount of indirect costs reimbursed to

GAO-13-760 NIH Indirect Cost Funding

universities.[24] This limitation only applies to higher education institutions, as stated in OMB Circular No. A-21.

A university submits a proposal to the federal agency responsible for negotiating a final rate—typically DCA. DCA reviews the submitted proposal and negotiates a final indirect cost rate with each university. DCA is responsible for providing technical assistance and guidance to the grantee community in developing indirect cost rate proposals, reviewing cost accounting practice disclosure statements, and negotiating and approving university indirect cost rates.

Proposed Changes to OMB Circular No. A-21

In February 2013, OMB issued proposed guidance that includes revisions to cost principles of OMB Circular No. A-21.[25] The proposed guidance reflects input from the federal and nonfederal financial community, including the Interagency Council on Financial Assistance Reform.[26] The proposed guidance would, among other things, allow more items to be directly charged rather than included as a component of the indirect cost rate.[27] As of September 2013, OMB had not issued final guidance.

---

[24]56 Fed. Reg. 50224 (Oct. 3, 1991) (relevant provision currently codified at OMB Circular A-21, G, 8, a).

[25]78 Fed. Reg. 7282 (Feb. 1, 2013).

[26]This Council included NIH and other federal agencies. It reviewed issues related to the application of OMB Circular No. A-21 for federally sponsored research at universities, including the administrative burden associated with current policies and costs. Specifically, the Council solicited comments from stakeholders and provided various recommendations to OMB for consideration in its proposed revisions.

[27]The proposed revision would include the costs of certain computing devices as allowable direct costs.

From 2002 to 2012, NIH Indirect Cost Reimbursements to Universities Increased Faster than for Direct Costs, with Most Going to a Small Number of Universities

From fiscal year 2002 to fiscal year 2012, NIH reimbursements to universities for indirect costs associated with NIH-funded extramural research increased at a slightly faster rate than those for direct costs, and during some portions of this period indirect cost growth increased notably faster than direct cost growth. In fiscal year 2012, the 50 universities with the largest research programs received over two thirds of total indirect cost reimbursement. Higher indirect cost rates tended to be associated with universities located in high-cost-of-living areas and privately owned universities.

From 2002 to 2012, Reimbursements for Indirect Costs Increased Slightly Faster than Those for Direct Costs, but Increased Notably Faster During Some Periods

Reimbursements for indirect costs from fiscal year 2002 through fiscal year 2012 increased slightly faster than reimbursements for direct costs, but increased notably faster during some periods. Over this period, NIH reimbursements for indirect costs grew by about 28.1 percent, from $3.6 billion to $4.6 billion.[28] Over the same period, NIH reimbursement for direct costs grew by about 27.0 percent, from $9 billion to $11.5 billion. However, because there were large differences between indirect and direct growth in some years, indirect cost reimbursements increased notably faster than direct cost reimbursements during some periods. For example, from fiscal year 2002 to 2003, the first year of this period, there was a large increase in direct costs that compensated for greater growth in indirect costs during other years. As a result, from fiscal year 2003 to 2012 indirect costs increased 16.9 percent, from about $3.9 billion to $4.6 billion, while direct costs increased 11.7 percent, from about $10.3 billion to $11.5 billion. Furthermore, in 6 of the 10 years, reimbursements for indirect costs increased relative to those for direct costs, by either increasing at a faster rate or declining at a slower rate. After fiscal year 2005, annual changes in reimbursements were generally small but consistent, with reimbursements for indirect costs increasing relative to direct costs in 5 of 7 years. (See fig. 2 for more details on the annual change in costs.)

---

[28]Our analysis generally focused on the relative differences between changes for indirect cost reimbursements and direct cost reimbursements. Therefore, we do not adjust the changes in reimbursements for inflation. Percentages are calculated based on the total amounts of reimbursement reported by NIH; the amounts of reimbursements in our narrative are rounded.

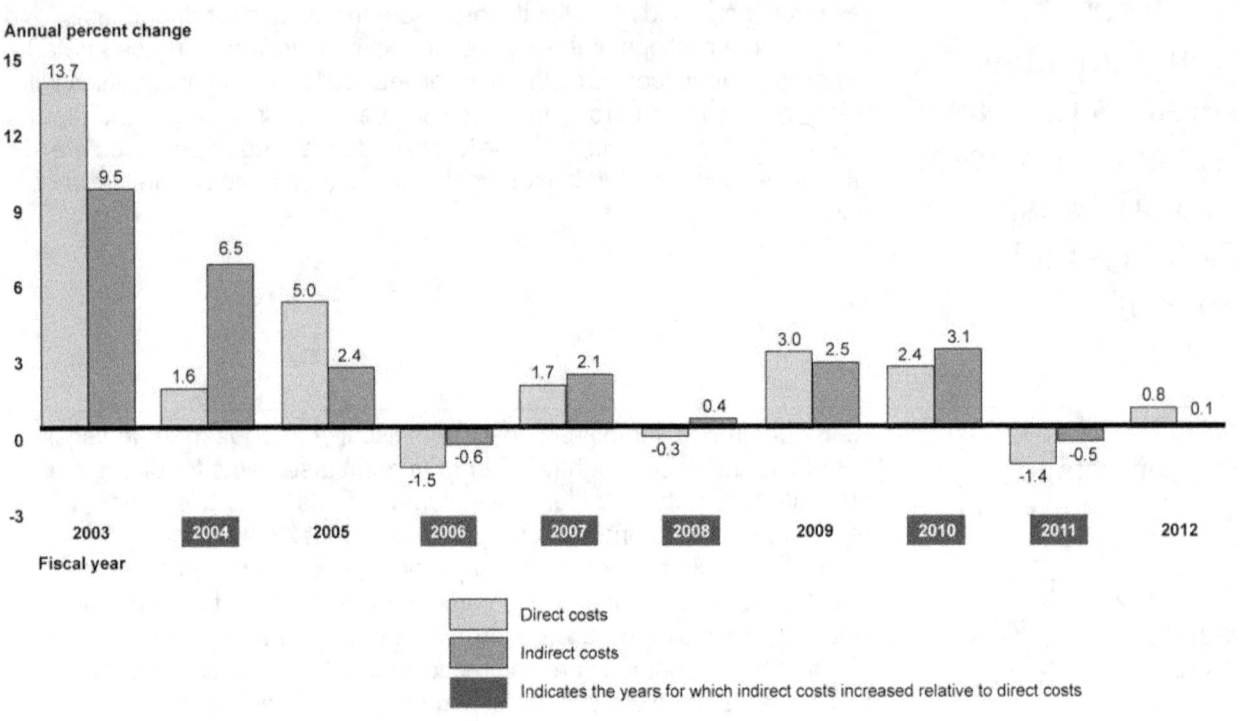

Figure 2: Percent Change from the Prior Year in Reimbursement for Direct and Indirect Costs, Fiscal Year 2003 to Fiscal Year 2012

Direct costs

Indirect costs

Indicates the years for which indirect costs increased relative to direct costs

Source: GAO analysis of NIH data.

NIH officials noted that, historically, NIH's reimbursements for indirect costs have remained a stable percentage of NIH's total funding for all NIH awards overall. Our analysis specifically for university research, which accounted for almost two-thirds of NIH's funding for extramural research in fiscal year 2012, indicates that in 2003 about 27.7 percent of NIH reimbursement for university research was for indirect costs, and in 2012 this percentage increased slightly to 28.6 percent. This occurred while NIH's budget for extramural research conducted at universities—which needs to cover both the direct and the indirect costs of research—slowed in the last few years. For example, during the most recent 5 years (fiscal year 2008 to fiscal year 2012), NIH's total funding for extramural research conducted at universities increased about 5 percent, whereas it had

GAO-13-760 NIH Indirect Cost Funding

increased about 21 percent in the 5 previous years (fiscal year 2002 to fiscal year 2007).[29]

In 2012 the 50 Universities with the Largest Research Programs Received Most of the Indirect Cost Reimbursements

In fiscal year 2012, almost 70 percent of NIH indirect cost reimbursement to universities was provided to about 10 percent of the universities (50 of a total of about 500) receiving NIH funding for extramural research.[30] (See app. I for the indirect cost reimbursements for these top 50 universities.) These top 50 universities had the largest research programs, as defined by the largest amount of reimbursement for direct costs and a relatively large number of research grants.

Indirect cost rates varied among these top 50 universities with the largest research programs, and the highest indirect cost rates were for privately owned universities and those located in high-cost-of-living areas. The indirect cost rates among the 50 universities ranged from 46.5 percent to 69.5 percent.[31] For the top 50 universities, higher indirect cost rates tended to be associated with universities in high-cost-of-living areas[32] and privately owned universities. For example, 8 of the 10 universities with the highest indirect cost rates were in areas with above-average costs of living, and 9 of the 10 universities with the highest rates were private. Some stakeholders reported several other factors that may be associated with variation of indirect cost rates among the top universities, including whether a university had a medical school or was receiving a utility cost

---

[29]This change in reimbursement for extramural research includes only research grants awarded to universities, and does not include training grants.

According to NIH officials, the difference between the increases in direct and indirect costs during the period from fiscal year 2002 to fiscal year 2007 and the increases in these costs from fiscal year 2008 to fiscal year 2012 was due in part to NIH's budget doubling in fiscal years 1999 through 2003.

[30]NIH provided direct and indirect cost data for 802 universities that received extramural research funding from fiscal year 2002 to 2012.

[31]Indirect cost rates for 5 universities out of the top 50 were not available from DCA.

[32]We measured local cost of living using the U.S. Census Bureau's "cost of living index" for 2010, which measures relative price levels of consumer goods and services in participating areas at a single point in time. Localities get a score between 82.8 and 216.7; the higher the score, the higher the cost of living. We defined high cost of living as an index of greater than 120.

adjustment.[33] Table 1 shows the characteristics of the 10 universities with the highest indirect cost rates among the 50 universities receiving the highest amounts of indirect cost reimbursement in fiscal year 2012. Among the 10 universities in the table, those with the highest indirect cost rates were Mount Sinai Medical School and New York University School of Medicine; Johns Hopkins University and Yale University had the largest research programs as measured by the number of NIH grants awarded.

---

[33]Certain universities are eligible for a rate increase of 1.3 percent to account for the cost of utilities. This rate increase is known as the utility cost adjustment.

Table 1: Characteristics of the 10 Universities with the Highest Indirect Cost Rates among the 50 Universities Receiving the Highest Amounts of Indirect Cost Reimbursement, Fiscal Year 2012

University	Final negotiated indirect cost rate (%)	Amount of indirect cost reimbursement ($millions)	Number of NIH grant awards	Cost of living index[a]	Type of institution	University is or has a medical school (yes or no)	Eligible for the utility cost adjustment[b] (yes or no)
Mount Sinai School of Medicine	69.5%	$55.3	380	216.7	Private	Yes	Yes
New York University School of Medicine	69.5	54.5	344	216.7	Private	Yes	Yes
Weill Medical College of Cornell University	69.0	35.6	257	216.7	Private	Yes	Yes
A bert Einstein College of Medicine, Yeshiva University	66.0	53.1	353	159.0	Private	Yes	Yes
Yale University	65.6	114.1	839	122.1	Private	Yes	Yes
University of Massachusetts Medical School, Worcester	64.5	44.3	335	103.3	Public	Yes	Yes
Boston University Medical Campus	63.5	29.1	241	132.5	Private	Yes	Yes
University of Southern California	63.0	56.4	352	136.4	Private	Yes	Yes
Johns Hopkins University	62.0	171.8	1,227	119.2	Private	Yes	Yes
Harvard University	61.5%	$55.1	111	132.5	Private	Yes	Yes

Source: GAO analysis of N H and Division of Cost Allocation (DCA) data.

[a]We measured local cost of living using the U.S. Census Bureau's "cost of living index" for 2010, which measures relative price levels of consumer goods and services in participating areas at a single point in time. Localities get a score between 82.8 and 216.7; the higher the score, the higher the cost of living.

[b]Certain universities are elig ble for a rate increase of 1.3 percent to account for the cost of utilities. This rate increase is known as the utility cost adjustment.

GAO-13-760 NIH Indirect Cost Funding

Stakeholders Identified Factors Related to Facilities and Administrative Costs That May Increase Reimbursements for Indirect Costs, but NIH Has Not Assessed Their Potential Impact

Stakeholders—university officials, DCA officials, and others—whom we interviewed identified several key factors that may lead to increases in reimbursements for indirect costs provided to universities. Some factors are related to the facilities costs, and others are related to administrative costs. NIH has not assessed the potential impact of future increases in indirect costs on its research mission, including planning for how to deal with these potential increases.

Uncapped Facilities Component of the Indirect Cost Rate Provides Few, If Any, Incentives to Control Costs

Some stakeholders underscored the importance to the research effort of providing funding for the costs of facilities. They explained that reimbursements for the facilities component of indirect costs—such as the amount of reimbursable square footage, operations and maintenance, building depreciation, and interest costs—help to support research innovation by providing funding for the development and maintenance of state-of-the-art research facilities. Some university officials we interviewed noted that these research facilities are necessary for conducting innovative biomedical research, such as research devoted to the role of genetic mutation for breast cancer that uses advanced lab space and equipment. They also noted that costs for these facilities have increased over time as biomedical research has become increasingly sophisticated. For example, a university's officials stated that from fiscal year 2002 to fiscal year 2009, the cost of its facilities to support research—including those used to support advancement in data and computing—has grown from about $88 million to about $145 million.

DCA officials stated that the uncapped facilities component of the indirect cost rate provides universities few, if any, incentives for controlling these potentially increasing costs. For example, DCA officials noted that there is no limit on reimbursement for interest costs under the facilities component. DCA officials stated that while reimbursements for interest costs may allow universities to support needed renovations or construction of new facilities, the fact that these reimbursements are not capped may also encourage universities to borrow money to build new facilities, which could lead to the building of more new space than is necessary for research needs. Officials also noted that these interest costs are out of DCA's control and may vary. For example, at the time of our work, interest rates—which are used to determine interest costs—were very low, but they could increase over time, which could increase costs for ongoing building projects or buildings that have already been completed, regardless of future building decisions by universities. Because of this factor, the indirect cost rate could be expected to increase, resulting in a potential increase in the amount of indirect cost reimbursements provided by NIH.

In addition, some stakeholders noted that, at the time of our work, 65 of about 500 universities receiving reimbursement for indirect costs in fiscal year 2012 were eligible for a rate increase of 1.3 percent to account for the higher cost of utilities.[34] DCA officials added that OMB's proposed revisions to Circular No. A-21 would allow all universities to receive some reimbursement for utility costs based on a revised formula. As a result, NIH reimbursements for indirect costs could be expected to increase as more universities would be eligible to include this cost in their indirect cost rates.

Administrative Cap Controls Potential Increases in Cost Reimbursement due to Growth in Administrative Costs Incurred by Universities

Some stakeholders noted that while the cap on the reimbursement rate for administrative costs—26 percent—helps to control reimbursements for indirect costs, it does not account for the recent increases in administrative costs reportedly incurred by universities. For example, university officials explained that their administrative costs have increased in order to comply with recent changes in regulatory reporting requirements, such as those related to reporting conflicts of interest. Some university officials explained that they have hired additional full-time staff to review and manage various reporting requirements as well as invested in additional information technology (IT) to support new software

---

[34]The utility cost adjustment was implemented in 1998 to replace a system of special utility cost studies. It was made available to 65 institutions identified in Exhibit B of OMB Circular No. A-21, based on whether they had submitted a special study in their most recent indirect cost rate proposal. Universities on the list receive this adjustment in addition to the utilities portion of indirect costs that a school negotiates based on its proposal. Although OMB Circular No. A-21 states that, beginning in July 2002, federal agencies must reevaluate periodically the eligibility of institutions to receive the utility cost adjustment, no changes have been made to the list since the utility cost adjustment was implemented in 1998, as we reported in 2010.

related to regulatory requirements. Additionally, some stakeholders noted that administrative costs also have increased due to trends in the way biomedical research is conducted, such as an increase in collaboration between universities in research studies and an increased use of IT for biomedical research. For example, some university officials explained that many biomedical research projects now use advanced technology—such as high-sequencing technology or imaging—that requires greater investment in computing resources by the university. Additionally, one university's officials noted that the advancements in IT provide support for interconnectivity, complex data security and data privacy requirements, and requirements for long-term storage and maintenance of electronic data. According to university officials at another university, in some instances they may charge some advanced computing equipment as a direct cost because it is specifically related to research; however, in most instances these computing resources are included in the administrative component of the indirect cost rate.

According to DCA officials, if costs that are part of the capped administrative component increase significantly, indirect cost reimbursements overall could increase if universities begin to categorize some of the costs as part of the uncapped facilities component. Specifically, DCA officials explained that currently there is a provision in Circular No. A-21 that advises certain limits on changing the categorization of certain costs—such as those costs incurred by a university that are associated with increased use of information technology—from the administrative to the facilities component. However, they noted that the proposed revisions to Circular No. A-21 did not include such a provision. DCA officials stated that they may be limited in their ability to control increases in reimbursements associated with these categorization changes if this provision is removed and if university administrative costs continue to increase.

NIH Has Not Assessed the Potential Impact of Increases in Indirect Costs on Its Mission

NIH has not assessed the potential impact of future increases in indirect costs on its research mission, including planning for how to deal with potential future increases of these costs. As we previously reported, NIH has a program to periodically identify, analyze, and manage significant risks to its objectives, strategy and mission.[35] NIH officials noted that they

---

[35]See GAO-09-687.

assess risks related to all extramural research funding as part of this program, and that this assessment does not specifically focus on indirect costs for universities. According to NIH officials, NIH has not conducted such planning because overall indirect costs have remained around 27 percent of NIH's total budget for all extramural research, and, in their opinion, future cost increases are unlikely to change this figure significantly in spite of factors that may contribute to increased indirect costs.

Therefore, NIH officials stated that they do not anticipate the need to consider adjusting reimbursements for indirect costs for most grants below the amount determined by a university's negotiated indirect cost rate, which would require a change in law or regulation.[36] However, NIH officials told us that should indirect costs rise significantly, they may need to reduce the number of research projects, which have already been reduced in part because of budget limitations and increases in the direct costs of research. NIH noted that the reduced budget in fiscal year 2013 resulted in 700 fewer individual research grants. Even at current levels, indirect costs constitute a significant portion of NIH's budget at about 20 percent. Therefore, over time, increases in indirect costs could cause further reductions in the number of research projects that NIH could support.

Conclusions

NIH has indicated that NIH funding for both the indirect and the direct costs of university research provides critical support for biomedical research, covering the indirect costs of operating a research institution and the direct costs of specific research projects. NIH faces uncertainty related to the potential impact of increasing indirect costs on its funding of future research. Among research grants to universities specifically, NIH's indirect costs are increasing at a faster rate than direct costs. While changes in recent years have generally been small, annual changes in reimbursement for indirect costs have consistently increased relative to those for direct costs, by either increasing at a faster rate or declining at a slower rate. Further, this has occurred while the growth in NIH's budget for extramural research has slowed in recent years, putting pressure on NIH to find ways to continue to maximize its support of innovative

---

[36]As previously noted, while OMB Circular No. A-21 requires agencies to adhere to the negotiated rate while it is in effect, an agency may apply a different rate when required by law or regulation. (OMB Circular A-21, G,11, b.)

GAO-13-760 NIH Indirect Cost Funding

biomedical research. Several factors are expected to contribute to future growth in indirect costs for NIH. These factors include that NIH's current system of reimbursing indirect costs—through indirect cost rates for each university calculated according to OMB guidance—provides few, if any, incentives for universities to control facilities costs. At the same time, the cost of university facilities to support biomedical research is increasing over time, as cutting-edge research requires more advanced labs and equipment.

NIH has not made plans for options that might address these trends—in part because it views increases in indirect costs as having been modest. However, indirect costs already represent one-fifth of NIH's overall budget and about one-quarter of NIH's budget for extramural research. NIH has experienced small but consistent increases in indirect costs, and factors suggest that indirect costs could increase more quickly over time in the future. If so, such increases could have an effect over the long term on the number and size of research grants that could be funded, thus posing a risk to scientific discoveries and knowledge.

Recommendation

To help address the uncertainty NIH faces related to the potential impact of increasing indirect costs on its funding of future research, we recommend that the Director of NIH assess the impact of growth in indirect costs on its research mission, including, as necessary, planning for how to deal with potential future increases in indirect costs that could limit the amount of funding available for total research, including the direct costs of research projects.

Agency Comments and Our Evaluation

We provided a draft of this report to HHS, and HHS provided written comments (reprinted in app. II). HHS also provided technical comments, which we incorporated as appropriate.

HHS indicated that it agreed with our recommendation and that NIH had already taken steps to implement it, but HHS disagreed with a number of our conclusions. Specifically, HHS stated that NIH assesses the impact of indirect costs through its annual budget projections, through planning and congressional justifications, and as part of its risk management program. The draft report acknowledged NIH's efforts in assessing risk facing its extramural research program. However, NIH has not indicated how these actions would address our recommendation by assessing the potential ongoing impact of indirect costs for universities on its funding of future research. Moreover, NIH has not developed a plan for how to deal with potential continuing increases in indirect costs for universities. Instead, HHS indicated that, in past years, increases in indirect costs have been proportionally consistent with increases in direct costs, and therefore, there is not an immediate risk to NIH's research portfolio. While the draft report acknowledged that indirect costs have remained a stable percentage of NIH's overall research costs, it also noted that, for universities—which received almost two-thirds of NIH's funding for extramural research—indirect costs increased notably faster than direct costs during some recent periods. Further, as indicated in the draft report, there are multiple indications that, for universities, indirect costs are likely to increase at a faster rate in the future, so past stability may not be sustained in future years. We remain convinced that increases in indirect costs could have an effect over the long term on the number and size of research grants that could be funded, thus posing a risk to scientific discoveries and knowledge.

In addition, in its comments, HHS included an analysis of indirect costs over the past decade for its overall extramural research portfolio. This analysis was different from our analysis because it focused generally on extramural research rather than specifically on university research. As noted in the draft report, our research questions were focused specifically on universities. Moreover, as institutions of higher education, universities generally have a broader focus on education than research institutions. Further, as noted in the draft report, universities are subject to OMB Circular No. A-21 and their administrative costs are capped, unlike other research institutions. Because of the unique issues that universities face, our analysis of indirect costs excluded nonuniversity research institutions to avoid the possibility of data from these other NIH grantees masking trends for universities, which are the recipients of the largest portion of NIH's grant funding.

Finally, HHS stated that we did not provide an opportunity for the department to provide input on our review of NIH's assessment of the potential impact of indirect costs on NIH's research mission. We disagree with this characterization. NIH provided input on this issue to us during three separate meetings. For all three meetings, we provided discussion questions in advance. During one of the meetings, we and NIH officials discussed the key facts that were to be included in the draft report, including this issue. In addition, we offered NIH officials the opportunity to provide additional information in writing, as appropriate.

As agreed with your office, unless you publicly announce the contents of this report earlier, we plan no further distribution until 30 days from the report date. At that time, we will send copies of this report to the Secretary of the Department of Health and Human Services, the Director of the National Institutes of Health, and other interested parties. In addition, the report will be available at no charge on GAO's website at http://www.gao.gov.

If you or your staff have any questions about this report, please contact me at (202) 512-7114 or at kohnl@gao.gov. Contact points for our Office of Congressional Relations and Office of Public Affairs can be found on the last page of this report. Other major contributors to this report are listed in appendix III.

Sincerely yours,

Linda T. Kohn
Director, Health Care

Appendix I: Indirect Costs and Rates for the Top 50 National Institutes of Health—Funded Universities, Fiscal Year 2012

University	Reimbursement for indirect costs ($)	Indirect cost rate (%)
Johns Hopkins University	$171,842,189	62.0%
University of Pennsylvania	132,558,612	60.0
University of Michigan at Ann Arbor	128,851,678	55.5
University of California San Francisco	123,730,058	54.5
University of Pittsburgh at Pittsburgh	115,284,723	51.5
University of Washington	114,508,104	54.0
Yale University	114,126,199	65.5
University of California at San Diego	107,909,828	54.5
Stanford University	101,755,908	n/a
Duke University	101,094,258	57.0
Washington University	100,949,670	52.0
University of California Los Angeles	92,485,025	54.0
Vanderbilt University Medical Center	89,397,501	56.0
University of North Carolina Chapel Hill	89,328,438	48.0
Columbia University Health Sciences	88,890,770	60.0
Emory University	74,684,383	55.0
University of Minnesota Twin Cities	66,118,864	52.0
University of Wisconsin Madison	60,091,265	50.5
University of Southern California	56,436,393	63.0
Mount Sinai School of Medicine	55,349,423	69.5
Harvard University[a]	55,128,269	61.5
New York University School of Medicine	54,484,823	69.5
A bert Einstein College of Medicine, Yeshiva University	53,081,812	66.0
Oregon Health and Science University	51,944,196	54.0
University of Texas Southwestern Medical Center—Dallas	51,217,775	58.5
University of California Davis	50,658,691	53.5
University of Chicago	50,134,610	57.0
Baylor College of Medicine	48,366,907	56.5
University of Alabama at Birmingham	47,643,167	46.5
Northwestern University at Chicago	47,324,211	54.5
University of Texas MD Anderson Cancer Center	46,842,255	—[b]
Case Western Reserve University	46,746,052	57.0
University of Colorado Denver	46,231,183	53.0
University of Iowa	45,128,057	51.0
University of Massachusetts Medical School Worcester	44,347,569	64.5

University	Reimbursement for indirect costs ($)	Indirect cost rate (%)
University of Rochester	43,942,735	54.5
Ohio State University	39,755,792	52.5
University of Illinois at Chicago	38,574,578	n/a
University of Maryland Baltimore	38,569,736	48.0
University of Utah	37,945,477	49.5
Weill Medical College of Cornell University	35,555,472	69.0
University of Miami School of Medicine	33,617,736	53.0
University of California Irvine	32,851,174	53.0
Indiana University—Purdue University at Indianapolis	32,389,023	55.0
Massachusetts Institute of Technology	31,992,836	n/a
University of Virginia Charlottesville	31,890,011	54.0
University of California Berkeley	30,868,910	53.5
Boston University Medical Campus	29,091,950	63.5
University of Florida	28,396,985	46.5
Cleveland Clinic Lerner College/Med-CWRU	$26,451,255	n/a

Source: GAO analysis of N H and Division of Cost Allocation (DCA) data.

Note:

n/a = not available: this institution does not negotiate its indirect cost rate with DCA.

[a]Harvard University negotiates three separate rates—one for the university, one for its School of Public Health, and one for its Medical School. The information reported here is for the university.

[b]While NIH classifies this institution as a university, it is classified by DCA as a hospital. Therefore, a rate is not available because hospitals have a different rate-setting process than universities.

Appendix II: Comments from the Department of Health and Human Services

DEPARTMENT OF HEALTH & HUMAN SERVICES

OFFICE OF THE SECRETARY

Assistant Secretary for Legislation
Washington, DC 20201

AUG 3 0 2013

Linda Kohn
Director, Health Care
U.S. Government Accountability Office
441 G Street NW
Washington, DC 20548

Dear Ms. Kohn:

Attached are comments on the U.S. Government Accountability Office's (GAO) report entitled, "Biomedical Research: NIH Should Assess The Impact on Its Mission of Growth in Indirect Costs" (GAO-13-760).

The Department appreciates the opportunity to review this report prior to publication.

Sincerely,

Jim R. Esquea
Assistant Secretary for Legislation

Attachment

GENERAL COMMENTS OF THE DEPARTMENT OF HEALTH AND HUMAN SERVICES (HHS) ON THE GOVERNMENT ACCOUNTABILITY OFFICE'S (GAO) DRAFT REPORT ENTITLED, "BIOMEDICAL RESEARCH: NIH SHOULD ASSESS THE IMPACT ON ITS MISSION OF GROWTH IN INDIRECT COSTS" (GAO-13-760)

The Department appreciates the opportunity to review and comment on this draft report.

GAO Recommendation: To help address the uncertainty NIH faces related to the potential impact of increasing indirect costs on its funding of future research, we recommend that the Director of NIH assess the impact of growth in indirect costs on its research mission, including, as necessary, planning for how to deal with potential future increases in indirect costs that could limit the amount of funding available for total research, including the direct costs of research projects.

HHS Response: HHS concurs with the GAO's recommendation. Furthermore, NIH has already implemented the recommendation. Assessing the impact of F&A costs has always been a significant consideration and part of the NIH annual budget projections, planning and congressional justifications, as well as part of our risk management program. Indirect costs are a necessary cost of doing scientific research, and NIH considers the total cost of a grant (direct and indirect costs) when determining the amount of each grant awarded. Further, it is important to note that long-term trends and prior analysis conducted by NIH indicate that indirect costs have been a proportionally consistent part of the overall NIH budget for more than two decades. Accordingly, we conclude that the risk of growth in indirect costs adversely impacting the research mission and funding available for research is low.

GAO's recommendation emanates from statements in the report that NIH has not assessed the potential impact of increases in indirect costs on its research mission. However, this objective was not included as part of the GAO notification letter and we did not have the opportunity to provide input on this objective during the field work phase of this engagement. The following general comments describe the efforts we have taken to assess the impact of indirect costs on our agency budget.

NIH Conducted Assessments of Indirect Costs

GAO concludes on pages 18-19 that the risk assessments NIH performs under our agency's risk management program do not address indirect costs or their potential impact. To the contrary, NIH has a comprehensive risk management program that addresses significant risks to its ability to achieve its mission. We continually evaluate numerous risks during the process of planning NIH extramural funding decisions, which includes assessing total costs of awards (direct and indirect costs) that encompass the ever-changing environment and emerging issues.

With respect to the risk of growth in indirect cost rates, the Department of Health and Human Services Division of Cost Allocation (DCA)—the entity responsible for reviewing indirect cost rate proposals and negotiating indirect cost rates for each of the universities for which it is responsible—states that rising indirect cost rates should not be a substantial immediate risk to the federal government because indirect cost rates are normally set on a predetermined basis and are negotiated on a three- to four-year basis. Further, as required by the cost principles, the negotiated indirect cost rate in effect at the time of award to be used for the life of the award effectively eliminates any potential risk to a grant award that the indirect cost rate will increase.

1

**GENERAL COMMENTS OF THE DEPARTMENT OF HEALTH AND HUMAN
SERVICES (HHS) ON THE GOVERNMENT ACCOUNTABILITY OFFICE'S (GAO)
DRAFT REPORT ENTITLED, "BIOMEDICAL RESEARCH: NIH SHOULD ASSESS
THE IMPACT ON ITS MISSION OF GROWTH IN INDIRECT COSTS" (GAO-13-760)**

We disagree with GAO's conclusion that states, "NIH has experienced small but consistent
increases in indirect costs, and factors suggest that indirect costs could increase more quickly
over time in the future. If so, such increases could have an effect over the long term on the
number and size of research grants that could be funded." According to the available data,
indirect costs as a proportion of the NIH budget have remained below 30 percent over the last 25
years. NIH conducted this analysis of funding in 2010 as part of the Future of Biomedical
Research (FBMR) project. The NIH Deputy Director for Extramural Research presented the
results of this analysis at the December 2010 meeting of the Advisory Committee to the Director,
NIH. Further, in our recent FY 2014 Congressional Justification (see chart below), we noted that
indirect costs from FY 2002 to FY 2012 (the time period of GAO's review) remained at
approximately 27 percent.

FY 2014 Congressional Justification
Statistical Data -- Grants, Direct, and Indirect Cost Awarded
(Dollars in Thousands)

Fiscal Year	Direct Cost Awarded	Indirect Cost Awarded	Percent of Total		Percent Change	
			Direct Cost Awarded	Indirect Cost Awarded	Direct Cost Awarded	Indirect Cost Awarded
FY 2002	$12,822,068	$4,835,456	72.6%	27.4%	13.4%	11.7%
FY 2003	$14,445,631	$5,301,292	73.2%	26.8%	12.7%	9.6%
FY 2004	$14,892,783	$5,647,066	72.5%	27.5%	3.1%	6.5%
FY 2005	$15,419,089	$5,795,178	72.7%	27.3%	3.5%	2.6%
FY 2006	$15,219,138	$5,781,293	72.5%	27.5%	-1.3%	-0.2%
FY 2007	$15,387,745	$5,876,060	72.4%	27.6%	1.1%	1.6%
FY 2008	$15,295,950	$5,903,730	72.2%	27.8%	-0.6%	0.5%
FY 2009	$15,683,872	$6,027,543	72.2%	27.8%	2.5%	2.1%
FY 2010	$16,040,991	$6,193,567	72.1%	27.9%	2.3%	2.8%
FY 2011	$15,849,082	$6,173,769	72.0%	28.0%	-1.2%	-0.3%
FY 2012	$15,978,032	$6,182,900	72.1%	27.9%	0.8%	0.1%
FY 2013 Annualized CR	$16,058,190	$6,213,918	72.1%	27.9%	0.5%	0.5%
FY 2014 President's Budget	$16,165,258	$6,255,349	72.1%	27.9%	0.7%	0.7%

We have recently assessed the trend in increased application submissions for competing
applications for investigator-initiated research project grants (RPGs) (see more
at http://nexus.od.nih.gov/all/2012/08/09/more-applications-many-more-
applicants/#sthash.LBwbsV5z.dpuf). Our assessment shows an increasing trend in the amount of
direct costs requested during the time period FY 1998-FY 2011, from $4.4 billion in fiscal year
1998 to just over $13 billion in fiscal year 2011. The amount of money awarded to competing
applications during that time period increased from $1 billion to around $2 billion.

Driven by larger grant awards, the indirect costs proportionally increase as well. However, the
rate of growth of reimbursements of indirect costs differed from the growth rate in direct costs by
only 1.1 percent (28.1 vs. 27.0, respectively). As a result, indirect costs as a percentage of total
costs have changed very little, from 28.4 percent in FY 2002 to 28.6 percent in FY 2012.

2

**GENERAL COMMENTS OF THE DEPARTMENT OF HEALTH AND HUMAN
SERVICES (HHS) ON THE GOVERNMENT ACCOUNTABILITY OFFICE'S (GAO)
DRAFT REPORT ENTITLED, "BIOMEDICAL RESEARCH: NIH SHOULD ASSESS
THE IMPACT ON ITS MISSION OF GROWTH IN INDIRECT COSTS" (GAO-13-760)**

Additionally, when NIH assessed the potential impact of indirect costs, we came to a different
conclusion than GAO. NIH reviewed and analyzed the data set that the GAO used for its data
analysis to determine the reason for the differing conclusions. We determined that GAO looked
at a unique slice of NIH-funded entities (i.e., the data was limited to U.S. Domestic Institutions
of Higher Education). From our analysis, we found that as a percentage of all research grant
obligations, indirect costs to universities have actually decreased slightly, from 21.6 percent in
FY 2002 to 21.4 percent in FY 2012.

More detailed analysis and comments related to the data set provided to the GAO follow:

"From 2002 to 2012, Reimbursements for Indirect Costs Increased Slightly Faster Than Those
For Direct Costs, But Increased Notably Faster During Some Periods."

> In actuality, the rate of growth of reimbursements of indirect costs to universities differed
> from the growth rate in direct costs by only 1.1 percent (28.1 vs. 27.0, respectively). As a
> result, indirect costs as a percentage of total costs have changed very little, from 28.4
> percent in FY 2002 to 28.6 percent in FY 2012.

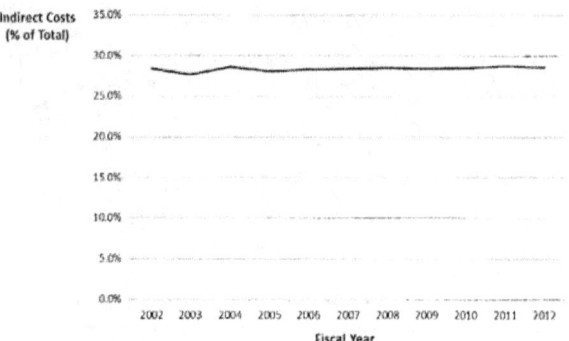

As a percentage of all research grant obligations, indirect costs have actually decreased slightly,
from 21.6 percent in FY 2002 to 21.4 percent in FY 2012.

3

**GENERAL COMMENTS OF THE DEPARTMENT OF HEALTH AND HUMAN
SERVICES (HHS) ON THE GOVERNMENT ACCOUNTABILITY OFFICE'S (GAO)
DRAFT REPORT ENTITLED, "BIOMEDICAL RESEARCH: NIH SHOULD ASSESS
THE IMPACT ON ITS MISSION OF GROWTH IN INDIRECT COSTS" (GAO-13-760)**

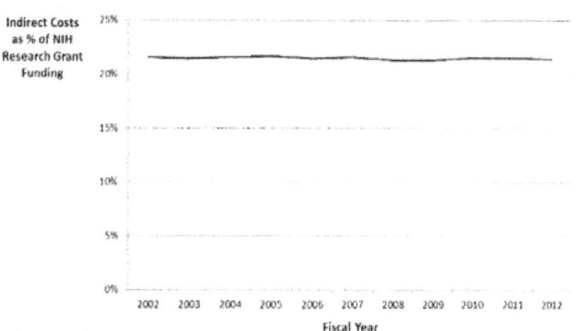

Where GAO states, "[f]urthermore, in 6 of the 10 years, reimbursements for indirect costs
increased relative to those for direct costs...," if there is no real difference in the growth rates of
direct and indirect costs, only random fluctuation, we would expect changes in indirect costs to
exceed changes in direct costs 50 percent of the time. Six of the 10 years is not statistically
significant from chance. Similarly, larger indirect cost increases in 5 of the last 7 years is not
statistically significant.

Furthermore, GAO states that "...in 2003 about 27.7 percent of NIH reimbursement for
university research was for indirect costs, and in 2012 this percentage increased slightly to 28.6
percent." Of the 11 years studied, FY 2003 had the lowest indirect cost percentage. The
percentage was higher in both the preceding and following years. In the following year, FY
2004, indirect costs represented 28.6 percent of reimbursements for university research, identical
to the percentage in FY 2012.

Lastly, GAO says "[i]n 2012, the 50 Universities with the Largest Research Programs Received
Most of the Indirect Cost Reimbursements. In fiscal year 2012 almost 70 percent of NIH
indirect cost reimbursement to universities was provided to 6 percent of the universities (50 of a
total of about 800) receiving NIH funding for extramural research."

These 50 universities received 70 percent of indirect cost reimbursement in FY 2012 because
they received 69 percent of the total funding to universities. These 50 institutions represent
about 10 percent of the 489 institutions funded (there were about 800 institutions that received
funding in at least one of the 11 years studied; only 489 received funding in FY 2012).

In FY 2012, about 95 percent of research funding to universities went to 150 institutions. The
distribution of indirect cost rates among the top 50 was similar to the overall distribution among
the 150 universities.

4

**GENERAL COMMENTS OF THE DEPARTMENT OF HEALTH AND HUMAN
SERVICES (HHS) ON THE GOVERNMENT ACCOUNTABILITY OFFICE'S (GAO)
DRAFT REPORT ENTITLED, "BIOMEDICAL RESEARCH: NIH SHOULD ASSESS
THE IMPACT ON ITS MISSION OF GROWTH IN INDIRECT COSTS" (GAO-13-760)**

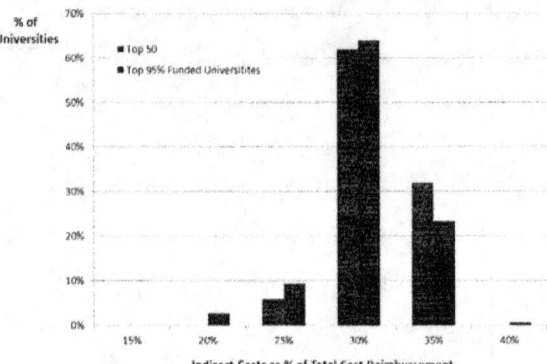

5

Appendix III: GAO Contact and Staff Acknowledgments

GAO Contact	Linda T. Kohn, (202) 512-7114 or kohnl@gao.gov
Acknowledgments	In addition to the contact named above, Will Simerl, Assistant Director; N. Rotimi Adebonojo; George Bogart; Amy Leone; and Roseanne Price made key contributions to this report.

GAO's Mission	The Government Accountability Office, the audit, evaluation, and investigative arm of Congress, exists to support Congress in meeting its constitutional responsibilities and to help improve the performance and accountability of the federal government for the American people. GAO examines the use of public funds; evaluates federal programs and policies; and provides analyses, recommendations, and other assistance to help Congress make informed oversight, policy, and funding decisions. GAO's commitment to good government is reflected in its core values of accountability, integrity, and reliability.
Obtaining Copies of GAO Reports and Testimony	The fastest and easiest way to obtain copies of GAO documents at no cost is through GAO's website (http://www.gao.gov). Each weekday afternoon, GAO posts on its website newly released reports, testimony, and correspondence. To have GAO e-mail you a list of newly posted products, go to http://www.gao.gov and select "E-mail Updates."
Order by Phone	The price of each GAO publication reflects GAO's actual cost of production and distribution and depends on the number of pages in the publication and whether the publication is printed in color or black and white. Pricing and ordering information is posted on GAO's website, http://www.gao.gov/ordering.htm. Place orders by calling (202) 512-6000, toll free (866) 801-7077, or TDD (202) 512-2537. Orders may be paid for using American Express, Discover Card, MasterCard, Visa, check, or money order. Call for additional information.
Connect with GAO	Connect with GAO on Facebook, Flickr, Twitter, and YouTube. Subscribe to our RSS Feeds or E-mail Updates. Listen to our Podcasts. Visit GAO on the web at www.gao.gov.
To Report Fraud, Waste, and Abuse in Federal Programs	Contact: Website: http://www.gao.gov/fraudnet/fraudnet.htm E-mail: fraudnet@gao.gov Automated answering system: (800) 424-5454 or (202) 512-7470
Congressional Relations	Katherine Siggerud, Managing Director, siggerudk@gao.gov, (202) 512-4400, U.S. Government Accountability Office, 441 G Street NW, Room 7125, Washington, DC 20548
Public Affairs	Chuck Young, Managing Director, youngc1@gao.gov, (202) 512-4800 U.S. Government Accountability Office, 441 G Street NW, Room 7149 Washington, DC 20548

Please Print on Recycled Paper.

www.ingramcontent.com/pod-product-compliance
Lightning Source LLC
Chambersburg PA
CBHW080640290526
45790CB00007B/3146